I LEANT UPON A COPPER PIPE

John Farquhar was born in Warrington, and educated at Liverpool University and St John's College, Oxford. He earned a modest but respectable living teaching English, French, German and Italian literature in various corners of the world. He now lives in Turin, Italy, where he visits museums, writes poetry, and enjoys ice cream.

He is the author of two previous books: *What to Expect When You're Dead*, a practical and informative guide to the afterlife, and *Hamstrung by Venus*, a somewhat polished collection of poetry. This, his third book, is by far his best.

I LEANT UPON A COPPER PIPE

WARRINGTON POEMS

by

JOHN FARQUHAR

VALLEY PRESS

First published in 2025 by Valley Press
Woodend, The Crescent, Scarborough, UK, YO11 2PW
valleypressuk.com

ISBN 978-1-915606-66-2
Cat. no. VP0254

Copyright © John Farquhar 2025

The right of John Farquhar to be identified as the author of this work has been asserted in accordance with the Copyright, Designs and Patents Act 1988.

All rights reserved. No part of this publication may be reproduced, stored in or introduced into a retrieval system, or transmitted in any form, by any means (electronic, mechanical, photocopying, recording or otherwise) without prior written permission from the rights holders.

Cover and text design by Jamie McGarry.

Printed and bound in Great Britain by
Imprint Digital, Upton Pyne, Exeter.

Contents

Preface   7

First Circle: The Hoagie Wagon   13
Circle Two: The Long Walk to Easement   19
Circle Three: The Lodging House   23
Circle Four: The Longford Lover   27
Circle Five: The Backs   30
Circle Six: Wilderspool   37
Circle Seven: The ABC Minors   43
Circle Eight: The Twelve Arches   49
Circle Nine: Fox Covert   56

Preface

These narrative poems are a celebration of working-class life in Warrington in the late sixties and early seventies. They are divided into nine 'circles', each circle starting from my house in St. Mary Street, and focusing on Warrington landmarks of importance to me as a child and young man: our outside toilet, the lodging house that was opposite my home, the Backs behind my home, Bridge Foot, Wilderspool Stadium, the ABC Cinema, the Hoagie Wagon, the Twelve Arches, and Fox Covert cemetery, where my parents are buried.

Whilst some of the incidents and observations may seem unflattering to the town, I am proud to be from Warrington. In one of my favourite comedies, Molière's *The Misanthrope*, the protagonist says that the more you love someone, the more you should point out their faults. This is what I have tried to do here. There is affection, nostalgia and love in the violence, the sarcasm and the anger. The events are exaggerated, but rooted in reality. They happened more than 50 years ago, but the spirit of the poem, it seems to me, is current.

You do not have to be from Warrington to understand these poems. Though it is unfashionable in modern writing, I have taken a series of particular events and tried to give them a general significance. I have also used the narrative form to tell stories in what I hope is an intriguing way; the same events and characters are visited and revisited, and viewed from differing angles to better understand them. A key word or phrase from one poem reappears in a different context in another. So, as well as a collection of poems, my book is a puzzle – but one that is not too hard to solve.

The book is also, in a sense, a memoir, in that someone vaguely resembling myself pops in and out, guides and cajoles the reader, tries to say something worth saying. I see it more, though, as a tribute to the Spirit of Warrington, to the River Mersey, and to the friends I grew up with, some now sadly dead, whom I still cherish and – yes – love.

John Farquhar, July 2025

to Jack, Les, Steve, Mike, Alban, and Jimi Allen

Pray for the Wanderer. Pray for me.

First Circle: The Hoagie Wagon

Barred from The Feathers that Christmas Eve
when Sully got glassed by Jesus Christ
for putting his hand up the skirt of that leggy angel
Jesus was engaged to;
Noreen, her name was.
Nice girl. My mum knew her mum.
They had the two of us together
in the hospital we're heading for
and stayed friends ever since,
as mothers do, to share the joy and pain.

I've never been in an ambulance before,
never felt the force of a fist or glass
in my astonished face.
Even now, the blood's not mine,
I'm merely an observer.
The groans belong to Sully
whose pain is out of reach,
whose blood went unavenged by me;
I understand, but do not live the code.

Familiar sights flash by.
The nurse in uniform
looks as though she's stroking Sully's curls
picking bits of glass from his indignant skull.
I watch, and think of chimps.
The hospital arrives,
Sully's mum is waiting on the steps.
She kisses him and tells him off,
thanks me for being a friend,

wishes her only son were more like me;
less macho.

Elsewhere,
Jesus is in jail
protesting innocence
and the chivalrous protection of a maid
to no avail.

Hospitals scare me.
All these casualties of Christmas
make me restless:
but what a job the nurses have,
to repair the drunks
and wash away their vomit free of charge,
tug the toy from the nose of that snotty brat
comfort the mother whose mother's just died
in agony at Christmas,
face the blood and filth of humans at their worst
yet keep their love and sanity somehow
and show me my true mirror –
a handsome-on-the-surface Caliban
defined by my need to leave.

I watch and wait.
Boredom comes.
Beyond absurd.

Having had his stitches
and a warning
I leave Sully with the wounded
and return by foot to Bridge Street
mateless, pensive and alone.

There
I leant upon a copper pipe
as a grizzled, aged man in white
emerged on the balcony of the Lion Hotel
to contemplate and greet the revellers
and wave and bless them, after which
he unzipped with unwarranted pride
waggled it a little (don't we all)
and peed a stream a young man would be proud of
over and down, over and down
as a couple there below
with faltering steps and slow
(found to be too amorous in the dark
under Bridge Foot in that infamous park
by the police, opposed to outdoor bliss)
under-passed this sibilant arch of piss
oblivious in their own warm world of love
to this Christmas waterfall that once was beer.

Christmas comes but once a year.

As he was led away
I heard the clock on Sankey Street strike midnight
and knew for certain I'd miss Midnight Mass
or would only get there after the bell had rung,
that caused such communal shame to me and mine:
proof I did not now communicate with Christ
or any corporeal or spiritual being
but sat alone of all my family on the bench
exposed for what I had become:
a Host-Refuser:
Redeemerless Apostate of the North.

Didn't we tell you he'd turn, the silent one?
The quiet ones are always ... aren't they just?
Gentle as he is, there's something off about him ...

The hell with it, the hell, I thought
and left the madding crowd
to face Bridge Foot alone
where the River Mersey wonders if it's worth it,
tempted to renounce her struggle here and now
in Warrington, and stop the senseless flow for once and all;
weary, as the townsfolk are,
of all that life shows itself to not be.

The sea is twenty miles away
where all this silt meets all that salt
to no purpose whatsoever.
The Mersey Estuary's the end of dreams.
The river joins the sea and thinks: *so what?*

As I, the human, think:
This is Christmas, I won't throw up
despite eight pints and those salted peanuts
I'll be in Slater Street before the Offertory
and pass the black-roofed house my true love lived in
who broke my heart
to pass the time,
a weight she freed me from.

Perhaps I'll pause once more and bow my head
before the wall and weeds behind the church
where she anointed me
and everything seemed simple in her eyes
and all life's beautiful illusions possible

in the lonely alchemy and delusion of first love;
where I renounced the Church and all Her works
for something much more splendid and less pure.
Asperges me, domina, hyssopo!
For mine is not the kingdom.

Such were my worthless thoughts
when, before the bridge, I saw and smelt
the briny off-white smoke against the starless sky
and manger-like appearance
of the pit-stop for lonely gourmet drunks
that was in those dead times The Hoagie Wagon.

The Hoagie Wagon.
How have I survived it?
Arteries – take a bow, you amaze me.
The neon sign, the astonishing stink of brine,
the limitless choice of hot dog, or hot dog,
made the way they make them in the States
with gluttonous excess and self-abuse,
their smallest roll one full foot long
from whose off-white ends protrude
three so-called sausages
of dubious gender, and rank
dripping with God knows what
and extras if you dared.

I dared that night: oh, God, I dared!
Free at last from the bonds of reason
reciting Dante in Italian
united with my own primeval cause
joyously alone
genderless, perhaps,

I walked to the edge of the Mersey
where the varicose van was parked
and joined the sinners of my own free will
to cram my mouth with hoagie
even as the Host was being lifted
in Our Lady's, where I used to pray.

In full knowledge of sin
I confirmed my Fall
to the man in the van:
A hoagie with all the trimmings!

What the fuck are trimmings?
the hoagie man replied.

Circle Two: The Long Walk to Easement

When boyish Twiggy fought for women's rights
and urged men not to be so breast-concerned,
warned us of the tyranny of curves,
and taught the world that freedom is flat-chested;
while hairy hippies preached we'd all be cleansed
by the breaking water of Aquarius
baptizing upturned faces in a flood
of mystical pre-birth and liquid love;
the toilet that I used was still outdoors.

It took me ten more years of work and pain
to join the middle class and shit indoors
as decent humans do,
who go beyond the body to the stars
which Christian Brothers used to point me to
discouraging those vibrant fleshy thoughts
and telling me the road to Hell
was paved with tits and itches in the arse,

but every time they had me on the ropes
and made me think I too should be a priest
I used to think how they were born from sex
and underneath each cassock is a cock.

Our poor old body's been abused too long
but Dionysus is a god
and those who will not pay him due respect
are justly driven mad
by the very functions he controls
without which life could not exist on Earth.

So, dear Reader, here's the deal:
come chill your arse with me, then let it warm
as we go back to 1968
when pipes froze over in St. Mary Street
and Warrington was clogged, but undefeated
and, after a brave struggle with the frost
the River Mersey died and rose again
to wearily resume her endless toil:
shipping all our shit to Liverpool.

The long walk to easement was cruel that December.
The very newspapers we used to wipe our arse –
The Mirror or *The Sunday Post* –
froze in the recess along with those dead spiders
making it a Sisyphean task
once you'd snapped an icy page or two
and run it like an ice pop on your bum
to achieve the warmth and pliability of June;
worse still, the bare bulb that reminded me of *Callan*
(I used to swing it with my other hand)
gave no light when exposed wires froze
so you couldn't see there was no water in the bowl
just one tight-fitting glacier of ice
which made the flush redundant
if it even came
though fortunately, for family health and safety,
my father was the last to use it every night.

As for the shape and size of the cistern
and dangling chain, just watch *The Godfather* again
and Michael Corleone's frantic fumble for his weapon
before, behind, above, between, below
though any soul who dared press his poor hand

between that cistern and the white-washed wall
where I took countless craps once I could walk
would find worse than a loaded gun taped there.

The long walk to easement began with fish fingers
and chips, fried in oil the old-fashioned way,
oil that was changed, like a car, once a year –
so saturated they slid down with ease
into the stomach where bacteria waited
like starving young artists
whose work goes unnoticed
forming fresh turds day after day
moulding their shape and their size and their colour
like primeval potters working on clay
then sliding out with them into the bowel
down the white bowl then East to the Mersey
more with a whimper than with a whoosh.

What happens to turds became an obsession,
a thirst for real knowledge no teacher would quench.
I once got in trouble for asking if Jesus
sat on a khazi in Nazareth.

A few years before, in the first flush of childhood
when Cartesian dualism weighed on my mind
I dashed through the back gate to follow my turd
pulling my pants up as I raced through the Backs,
crossing myself in front of Our Lady's,
left at the top, along Knutsford Road,
following the unsensuous curve of the Mersey
right up to Bridge Foot and that sharp bend;
there, I just stopped and waited and looked
into the Mersey, expectantly.

If there are ghosts, there you will find me;
alone on Bridge Foot, the Mersey below
adapting the game I'd just learnt in school,
not as refined as Christopher Robin,
no donkey or bear, no need for a twig,
learning of life, the mind and the body
playing Warrington 'poo sticks', all by myself.

Cacophilia should not be condemned
in children at least, if we want them to learn.
Discover the body: discover yourself.
Cuius stercus bene olet
was the first Latin phrase to fire my mind
and lead me to Virgil, Catullus and Horace;
the Romans, as always, who shaped my young world
had a healthy respect for life's fluid meaning
as they sat side by side out in the open
on holes in the stone, fresh sponge in their hand
talking of Caesar while cleaning their arse;
plotting to kill his assassins, perhaps,
an image that sparked my long love of their culture
much more than *amo, amas, amat.*
The ancient Greeks, too, shat out in the open
without too much shame and no private doors
preparing the way for Democracy's truth:
which of these turds came out of a king?

I accept and embrace my bowel and my bum,
my brain and my piles,
the pain and the smiles,
the weirdness of life,
and when I want answers to where it's all at
I rejoice as I sit there, where Socrates sat.

Circle Three: The Lodging House

A woman and a man against a wall,
her legs around his calves,
his Charlie Chaplin trousers hanging down,
her knickers on the ground and skirt pushed up,
the bottle rolling round their destroyed shoes
staining the step with cheap red wine
dripping out unnoticed, undesired
as both of them defy the Lodging House
he's slamming her against to reclaim life
and shudder, to forget the pain of being poor
and filthy and despised by those
who have it off the decent way
at the proper time and place indoors
in bedrooms of their own
making love to Mozart
and bringing some decorum to a fuck.
To whit:

she opens her legs as flowers open,
he enters her vagina, not her cunt,
gives her seed, and doesn't 'shoot his load'
as the dosser from the Lodging House just has.
He shot his load inside her well and good
and may have knocked her up against a wall.
Could anything be more indecent?
Don't the poor have any shame at all,
to even take the chance to make more children?

Well, the dosser has zipped up
and handed back her knickers to his love.
They stay outside in silence and hold hands.

They look and smell as bad as you'd expect,
but the moon, the stars and universe above
make no judgement and feel no offence

as I, and all my street, judged and felt offended
by the flophouse, dosshouse, four-penny coffin,
call it what you will, that loomed at me
every time I opened my front door.
Worse than a workhouse
in its unclean parody of white
straight outta Dickens;
three crumbling stories high
with bricks as grey as corpses' cheeks
and beds for eighty Irishmen
who slept in day clothes every night
and stared at my old terraced house
through filthy, broken windows.

I couldn't look; I had to hold my nose
for we were the decent poor
on the right side of the street, with grids unblocked
and steps a depth of red you could take pride in.

The Lodging House was always there
like the threat of Hell
when I went to school or got the fish and chips
or chewed the fat with Mr. Lapp, who
didn't want the dossers in or near his shop:
the smell that lingered when they left
was very bad for business,
anything the lodgers may have touched
or seen or breathed on with their urine breath
might have to be marked down or sold at cost.

Why can't they knock it down? I used to think.
Not: *Which rich bastard built this pile of shit
and makes men live in slums while they grow fat?*
I thought the wrong way round, as I was meant to.
Slums are built in Paternoster Square,
Pater Noster: the choice of name should make you sick
or you've no conscience.
I had no conscience as a child,
I wanted the dossers dead, as we all did.
I prayed the Lodging House would disappear
as evil does in fairy tales;
I was a well-brought-up young boy,
the architects of poverty loved me.

The nightmare of the Lodging House
is back to haunt me in an unexpected way:
Nihil habet paupertas durius in se.
The winos, weirdos, atheists and addicts
I was warned against and wanted dead
seem to call now from untended graves
to say they too were human and had souls
that felt deep pain and needed love
and had hope once that didn't last
and didn't plan to live and die as dossers
on those bare and filthy mattresses I never saw,
too scared to go inside the Lodging House
turning up my educated nose,
condemning sinners from a distance
as all who believe in Heaven always will.

Who were the poor bastards
in that grim sixties workhouse?
Why didn't they smash my working-class windows in
when they looked onto the row of terraced houses

which must have seemed like palaces to them?
Why didn't we unite in common cause
against those with uncommon accents
who make men's misery their source of wealth?
The simple answer is the dossers were our bait and switch
who brought house prices down
(though we all rented ours)
and, for all our poverty, they were a source of secret pride:
at least we didn't stink as much as them.
We may have had a mouse or two
but all the rats stayed in the Lodging House.
Why would they want to move?

St. Mary Street is cleaner now.
The Lodging House has disappeared.
They knocked it down before it fell,
but the space it occupied
is still a space here in my mind
and I cannot forget
the crime against us it represented
or the simple fact that all the rich did
was use its bricks to build some other Hell.
Out of place. Out of mind.
Out of sight. Out of time.
The Lodging House is everywhere
and, with such an insufficiency of love
throughout the loveless, modern world
the Lodging house will rise again
and turn profit for some bastard
and none of this will ever end
until the poor twist their gnarled and calloused hand
out of the shape of the prayer that has failed them
into a fist that the rich understand.

Circle Four: The Longford Lover

The Longford Lover has called it a day.
His infamous dick, which parted more hair
than a barber's old comb is back in its lair
like Baby Jesus, asleep on white hay.

He used to have threesomes with young Latchford ladies
down by the locks of that once-grand canal.
He bedded two sisters just for a bet.
Praeceptor amoris, doctus amet.

While I would watch the pleasure boats bobble
on the wide water near my Latchford home
his arse was shafting
two thousand women
in the long grass, like a mad Irish gnome.

The Spirit of Warrington animates him:
he had sex in The Carlton, The Lion and Feathers,
sex in a toilet and sex on a wall,
sex in St. Mary's, St. Alban's, St. Oswald's,
sex under bridges, sex over all,

sex while stark naked or wearing a gown,
sex with young women who came to my town
from Wigan, St. Helens, Widnes and Crewe
to get the best sex that they ever knew.

He had sex on a table and sex in a chair,
sex at a wedding, a wake and a fair,
sex with a Swede and a German and Greek,

sex with the mighty, sex with the meek,
sex with triplets, twins and a clone
but claims to have never had sex on his own.

I love the guy, his tales and his music.
I know all the lyrics of 'Warrington Man'.
Let's all throw tomatoes at Wigan supporters
(forgetting to take them out of the can!)

He was the one who first conned Deep Purple
to raise the dead in the Lion Hotel.
He built a plaque where Keith Richards fell down.
He gave us such pride in our turbulent town.

No-one laughed louder, no-one smiled more,
no-one drank faster, nobody swore
with such vulgar dexterity, nobody gave
more life to my town
from Longford to Latchford
from cradle to grave.

He's hung up his cock to play snooker instead,
a decision young women in Widnes still mourn;
a town where the men are so clueless in bed
that most of the babies are Warrington born.

I bought him two drinks once (one was an insult)
there at the Union, where he was DJ
and watched as he downed them both in two minutes
and the walls to the sixties crumbled away.

The tales that he told had hips like Mick Jagger
and the subtle finesse of a Status Quo chord

but none of us spoke, and all of us listened.
In the Court of Great Sex, he was the Lord.

Did you really make love, Chris, to two thousand plus?
I hope that you did, but I really don't mind.
You made Warrington laugh, and were one of us
in music and life and love of mankind.

So, this poem is now yours, for all that it's worth.
Let's drink to the body and carnival mirth.
Two pints of mild, and balls to the bell.
Ale, and farewell, Chris. Ale, and farewell.

Circle Five: The Backs

I wasn't born the day they hauled away
the galvanized bomb shelter from the Backs
that kept St. Mary Street from Nazi bombs.
They took it to a tip
and crushed it like a can of coke;
and that was that.

I know from all my aunts that its main use
(before and after Hitler went to Hell)
was as a dance and concert hall
for under tens, supervised by older kids
who kept the profit from the penny paid
willingly, sometimes, by children from Our Lady's
and the other place, where I was later told
those freaks who do not cross themselves come from.
In terms of making money on the side
it was an MBA for some young guns.

My aunt found out first-hand in that bomb shelter
how tough the entertainment business is:
when she and he were both thirteen
a future businessman I shall not name
(*Nil nisi bonum*, after all)
taught her how impure pure Capitalists are –
she promoted the concert all week long,
he stood at the door and took the cash
(in every sense)
then legged it into Miller Street and safety;
so he thought,
but Hell had no fury like my fierce Aunt Hilda.

She found him guzzling Tizer from the takings
and gave him 'what for', in those days
when 'what for' was acceptable and good –
she did the only thing a woman could
in those dark, unequal times when men were men:
she beat the fizzing Tizer out of him.

All this was legend when I was a child
and the Backs had been restored to what I knew:
a piece of dirt behind our terraced house
to learn and live and win and lose and love,
the playing fields of Eton
without Eton, or their fucking boating song.

The Backs was just the size of a football pitch
and garages at either end the aluminium nets
that shook the street when goals were scored
with Judgement Day reverberations
which echoed through the thickest bedroom wall
and woke night workers up
who slammed their windows open
suggesting we could go to Vickie Park
which we never did
unless they came in rage through their back door
in seedy, unforgettable Y-fronts.

This is where we held Bonfire Night
before fireworks were sanitized
and permits were required
to celebrate on so-called public land.

Speaking of which,
at that time, we Catholics had no qualms

to throw a fellow Catholic on the fire.
He was just some guy we made together
and the flames devoured him so beautifully –
especially when we stuck those bangers in his pants
or concealed a rocket in his crotch,
which wasn't wise, but neither are the young
and you cannot live your life in a sheep pen.

I'm glad I'm not a kid today.
They're always looking down at some damn thing.
Looking down so much will make you blind
and you only start to live when you look up.

You only start to live when you look up.
Oh God, have I become the priest
the nun and brother prophesied?
Or have I just grown old?
A bit of both, I suppose.
Though spiritual in part,
the best of me
is a crochety old fart
and I embrace my flatulence with pride
as all old codgers should.
Wherever you be
on land or sea
always let your wind go free,
a poem my mother knew by heart
and loved.

Back to the other Backs:

I summon One-Eyed Martha from her grave;
the Gorgon of St. Mary Street,

gnarled fingers of white bone
turning babies into stone,
freezing children in mid air
with a single, death-like stare.

When boys and girls came out to play
she dragged the rotten wood of her back gate
across the cobble stones of her back yard
latched it to the toilet
and stood there by the wall, folding her terrible prongs
across that life-drained chest,
and stood there.

That was all she did, or had to do.
Stand. Fold arms. Just look. One eye.
Oh, Christ, don't look, or else you'll die!

Cullies missed and conkers cracked,
footballs self-deflated,
hop-scotch girls fell flat upon their face.
If blood was drawn, she smiled, and drank it in.
Her face was frost incarnate.
Her purpose in life was to stand on life's edge
and freeze it for the rest of us,
as we tried in vain to play and skip
and stay safe inside the circles
of the rope that beat against the dirt
while adulthood leered at us
in her joyless form and skinny legs
to trip us up and blood our knees
and tell us we would die some day,
for she was Death
and all she had to do was wait

silent at her worm-gnarled gate
sucking out our breath from where she stood
saying with her eyes: *you, too, are mine.*

She broke my best friend's leg once.
Fat Dave. Here's how she did it:

The Backs had seven garages in all.
The seven hills of Latchford, standing tall.
Two tailor-made to play football
while five stood in a line along a wall,
with two feet in between and six-foot drops
which we would leap across like mountaineers
yelling *Geronimo*, for no good reason.

The Council had condemned the garages
and put *no trespassing* on every one
which made them sacred in our eyes.
We wondered how to get inside.
The padlocks were too strong even for bangers.
Then, one day, Dave the fattest found a way;
when he wasn't looking, but *she* was.

One-Eyed Martha didn't like Fat Dave.
He farted in her face and often gave
her cat a diuretic in its saucer
and said the Mother's Union ought to force her
to take a witch-hood test, and maybe burn her
if such was still the law,
and Martha, normally so taciturn
called down this curse on Dave:
Fuck off, fat pig, I'll see you burn.

They were, in short, a movie by themselves
and we knew the showdown couldn't be far off.

One Sunday afternoon at three o'clock
Martha stood like a wrinkled siren on a rock
by her dried-up gate, scratching her licey hair
fixing us in her cold, cyclopic stare
as we prepared to leap the garage gaps,
Appo first, then Pee-Wee, me and Plunger,
Fat Dave the last, in loose and beltless jeans.

Before Fat Dave took off, he turned his back
to One-Eyed Martha, dropped his ample keks
and treated her to the fullest moon
a werewolf could ever howl to
staring at her through his hairy legs
with a cheeky, schoolboy grin.

Martha didn't blink, but slid her boney fingers
to her patch, and took it off,
revealing first to us a glassy bead
which she removed and lifted in the air
until it caught the sun whose rays
shone and shimmered on Dave's flabby arse
and seemed to burn him, for he leapt
high into the air and came crashing down full-length
which proved too much to bear for the garage
and Dave fell six foot under.

Fearful silence followed for some seconds
until we heard with great relief Dave's manly voice:
My fucking, shitting, bastard, bloody leg,
and knew he was in pain, therefore alive

and so we crowded gingerly
around the Dave-shaped hole
to peer down on him where he lay
his leg at quite an angle.
He looked up at me and I looked at the dirt
and empty garage, open to my eyes for the first time,
a sight I'd waited for for years, and thought:
There's nothing in there after all,
and part of childhood seemed to pass away
until Dave yelled: *Call a fucking ambulance you twat!*
which I did from Knutsford Road
for none of us had phones.

A plaster was put on Dave's flabby leg
and he was warned to keep his trousers on
and Martha told to keep her glass eye covered
which she did, and stood less often by the gate,
seeming not to need the Backs as much,
turning her one eye to TV inside
and when they came to knock our mountains down
I felt little, and the Backs for me
lost their purpose, and potency.

Circle Six: Wilderspool

If they lost a match I loved them more,
so by the first few weeks we were close friends
though, at that age, the most I ever did
was jump the two-foot wall with other kids
and shyly shake their massive, muddied hands
and tell them not to worry, and to rest:
they'd done their best; that's all a fan can ask.

They taught me how to deal with thwarted hopes
though mine would be the Oxford, bookish kind
and theirs was blazoned on their blooded shirts
looking down and sideways out of shame,
their wintry wisps of breath just hanging there
in such sad contrast to their massive lungs
and nothing left to do with all that pain
but fight and lose for twenty minutes more
because you simply cannot walk away
and Rugby League's a brutal family sport.

I didn't use to walk down Fletcher Street
or squeeze through clanking turnstiles with the rest,
I found an unofficial, rusty door
at the Railway End, my chosen spot
big enough to squeeze through for three years
till puberty attacked and wrecked my life,
and I had to pay a shilling to see the Wire lose.

My wanderings began at Wilderspool.
I found the town I called my home and loved
could never be my home for very long,
being where I didn't yet belong.

I watched, but didn't have the skill to play.
I spoke in northern vowels, but not the northern way,
preparing for my restless, rootless life.

It started early on, when I was ten:
we were being beaten by the Saints,
silence had descended on the Earth,
eight thousand shoulders dropped like Trojan walls
after the Trojan horse had done for them
when suddenly a small child sang:
Now, the Wire! Wire till I die!
His holy, piping, pleading voice
had all the futile innocence of youth
as it echoed through the silent stands,
then came the Saints supporters' jeers
piercing us like Grecian spears.

In the exposed corner where I stood
some laughed, some winced and others shook their head
but an old man in an older scarf
turned wistfully to me and simply said:
We used to win games when I was a lad.

Really? I replied,
not knowing yet the right response
to any affirmation at the Railway End
was: *Fucking hell!*

That one word – *really* – marks the point
I lost my sense of home
and is, I'm sure the sweet and bitter source
of that precocious essay on Camus
still hanging in the classroom, gathering awe.

It really caused a stir that day
at the Railway End.
Four lads nearby,
with sixteen plastic glasses at their feet
empty of beer, and bored by life
took a sudden interest in me:

What'd dee fuckin say?
Really! ... Really? ... Really! ... Fuckin ell!
Are you from Stockton Heath, yer little cunt?
No, St. Mary Street. It's just across the track ...
The track?
The fuckin railway line, the little fucker means.
The track? Who says the fuckin 'track'?
Fuckin Yanks. You a fuckin Yank?
No, I'm Warrington, born and bred.
Warrington, my arse.

Warrington, both then and now,
can never be my arse
which is why I wrote this poem
but, I digress.

The old man in a flat, outdated cap,
despite his bulbous nose and bird-like face,
wasted muscles, skinny arms and squint
became my bodyguard
and lifted Learning's cudgel high above his head:

Leave the lad alone, you uneducated twats.
If he don't speak like us he's got a chance.
This is why we voted Wilson in:
if he gets to leave this shithole good for 'im!

The mob was silenced for a moment, and dismayed
but rallied soon to Warrington's defence:

Warrington ain't a shithole ...
Longford is.
An' Orford.
Dallam in the dark.
Padgate in the morning.
But Warrington as a whole
is not a fucking hole ...

The old man must be dead some forty years.
I see his face as clearly as my own
and love him for his eloquent defence
of the wanderer I was and am and will be,
yet love the others, too, who stayed and lived and died
in Warrington
and never read a book in all their life.
Strange as it may seem, I wrote this poem
to toast their rich and unremembered souls.

This *really* moment, still alive for me
was brought to a glorious end
by a thump, and a slide and a thud.

What's that fucking noise?
Fuckin ell – Brian Glover's scored!
Brian Glover's scored?
We've missed it for another fuckin year.

Brian Glover was my hero.
A fat, unbalanced winger,
Warrington through and through,

brave and fierce and kind to me.
I have his autograph a dozen times.
No-one thudded into that stone wall
quite like Brian when he scored a try.

One more moment shaped my life that day
and taught me how in time
that which isn't yours in life
may become more precious, as a poem.

Although, on match day, I crawled across the track
looking left and right with proper care
in case the daily train's timetable had been changed
and entered Wilderspool illegally
to cheer the Wire on, without a hint of guilt
for I was very poor, and so were they,
when the match was done
I loved to join the human river surge
down Fletcher Street, and out onto the Causeway
and so I did that day
in bobble hat and scarf and gloves,
buoyed by the smell of beer,
delighting in the force and power of the crowd,
a mighty human torrent pouring through Bridge Foot
shaming the listless Mersey there below
which I would later watch with such deep sadness.

The sea of people parted
at the confluence with Knutsford Road.
The mainstream went by Cromwell's sordid statue
and headed to the first pubs in the town
but, I, a Latchford lad,
followed the smaller stream south
to Tizer, beans on toast, and Dr. Who.

This is when the incident occurred.

As I was about to make my turn
an ugly, pimpled Saints fan stole my hat,
yelled in inarticulate delight,
performed a strut
as primitive as his town:
a cultural and literal backwater
the Mersey has judiciously bypassed.
I was ten and he at least sixteen
and I could only freeze before such crime,
too shocked to even call for help or cry.

And yet, a second time that day,
a saviour came, uncalled for.

A blond-haired girl in a yellow top
and the shortest, bluest mini skirt I've seen
pulled back the thug by his red scarf
making him choke within the law
then kneed him where it hurts us to be kneed
until he dropped my hat to clutch his crotch
and left his manhood there to ridicule
and then she turned to me and smiled
a smile I'd give my life to see again,
replaced my hat, and gave me such a kiss
that time stood still.

Though she was just a moment of my life
and now girls offer me their seat on trains,
her breath is on my cheek as I write this;
her smile, her warmth, and mesmerizing legs
tell me life is good, and love exists.

Circle Seven: The ABC Minors

Before you knew it, an organ arose.
A Wurlitzer, or some kraut name,
and a bald man came to greet us like a god
playing with one hand and waving with the other
while we yelled our weekly solemn pledge
to the Children's Film Foundation
in vowels the Famous Five
would thoroughly disapprove:
even their dumb dog Timmy
spoke a crisper English than me
and my factory-fated mates
marked 'manual' at nine years old.
How they hated that bitch, Enid Blyton,
whom I pretended to hate.

But, what the fuck!
We were young
and suckers for a song
and so the rafters rose:

We are the boys and girls well known as
the minors of the ABC!
We all piss together
though the posh ones 'ave a pee!

Then the ones with birthdays went on stage
and nearly shat themselves if asked to speak
and got a balloon from some dysfunctional clown,
and other nonsense dragged the morning out
while the latest from the CFF was loaded up

telling tales of go-karts and the bravery of boys,
sometimes with a token girl
(though, thank God, not too often)
and as the wished-for darkness fell
we stuck deep in our gob
those gum-numbing penny ice lollies
shaped like rockets
called rockets,
three colours, all one flavour,
or threw them at the clown upon the stage,

and that was the rally of youth in those days.
A wild illusion of freedom for the poor:
three hundred screaming kids and one bald man
in Warrington each Saturday till noon
while our poor parents stayed in their sad bed
missing out on passion, love and joy,
wilting like lilies sold and grown for graves
though sometimes managing to make another baby
before they went to cash their green shield stamps.

Before the feature came the short
carried over from the other week
in which the hero – whose name meant nothing to us –
had been mangled, crushed, and generally killed
holding a coal mine up with his good hand
while lesser men escaped
or shoved off a cliff by a hideous cockney
to be impaled on jagged rocks below
or wrapped around a Blackpool tram
to save a blind boy and his careless dog.

Now, here he was again without a scratch.

Unkillable, as we were,
and how we cheered, unless some woman kissed him
at which point we pushed our little fingers down our throats
and gagged until a man got punched or shot
and sanity returned.

Who went with me?
God, I forget.
I remember the journey, but not who I travelled with.
Past the uncatholic school, up thirty grime-stained steps,
dodging death across the Causeway traffic
and down those steps again that led
to the seemingly solid black bridge
and that white, unsanitary foam, immobile on the Mersey.
The dizziness I felt as I looked down
and the mortal exaltation if a steam train passed
when I would stop and hang onto the other rail
and feel my soul shake with the bridge
as I became one with the water below
feeling the thrill of fear and pull of death,
as close to God at nine years old
as any human ever is
so that sometimes, having crossed the bridge
the other life the Ritz now represented
seemed gaudily insufficient
until I entered the velvety womb of the stalls
and opened up in manufactured darkness
to cinematic lies, as I still do.

Cinemas may come and go
but money never dies.
The ABC went bingo for a while
and the Ritz was resurrected
by two fat ladies, eighty-eight,

but long it could not last
for the seventies were sexy
in a way that bingo isn't
and bankers put their money
where their mouth would like to be:
in young girls' knickers
and the sweaty promise of a hot dance floor
and called it Mr. Smith's.

Mr. Smith's transformed my little town
into a den of thin equity
injecting her with lucre, and the rest:

the disco sound of '75
arrived in Warrington in '82
so the ABC was gutted to make way
for Donna Summer and her sort
and people came from Liverpool
to sweat and grind their youth away
in the hippest nightclub in the world
on the banks of the saddest river.

Yes, even I went there in '82
and – what may come as no great shock to you –
found I was not made for disco fever
or the joyous gyration of alpha male hips.
In all my life, the only thing I pulled
in Mr. Smith's was my calf muscle.
I'd nod and sidle up to girls, of course,
but the beat had me beaten from the start:

You what? You what? Speak up! Can't hear you!
Sometimes I saw a glimpse of raw pity.

Mostly indifference tinged with contempt,
and so I'd get drunk and sing inwardly:

Oh, fuck it! Oh fuck it! Farewell, northern maid.
Somewhere in here there's some big loud bastard
who'll yell in your ear before 2am
after he's ordered two pints for the road
and he'll stick his fat tongue in your delicate lobe
and his gross spider fingers will crawl over you
and a new life will come from the old,
at his place or yours or maybe outside
against the cold stone or in the dead grass
which leaves me unmanfully sad.

Vale, puella, at tu dolebis.

As couples paired off, I wandered alone
through what had been the Ritz to me,
haunted by the lack of joy
in this mind-numbing noise
and the loss of that wonderful wildness
that used to sanctify this place
where we launched rockets at bright, gaudy clowns.

How soon adult skin coils round your young neck
to choke the roar of childhood,
insinuating in you mature thoughts
of adult deeds, which soon become
the sad, solemn need to get your leg over
before you go back to the job that you hate.

As I moved through the throng
past Bogart-like bouncers

the sweat of the young
fell from the moist roof
into my beer with a sad, salty splash.
So I set down my glass and just left,
made the ten-minute walk
to the silence of Latchford
where dreams don't come true
but neither do lies.

When Mr. Smith's too began to lose money,
one night it burnt down, as such buildings will.
I heard the good news and ran to Bridge Foot
to pick up the rubble of so many moments
in a true pagan wasteland
while the Mersey stayed solid, indifferent and still.
The cinema has kept me alive
but I need to be nothing so badly sometimes.
The air that we breathe is so startlingly loveless,
the stars that we love indifferent and cold,
the song of the river is emptied of meaning,
the movies that formed me so terribly old.

Circle Eight: The Twelve Arches

And now I remember the age of steam.
The Mersey spanning arches where I sat
two foot from the railway line
to watch doomed giants bellow out their last
in magnificent defiance of the times,
the last great wonders of my childhood world
before it tottered to efficiency and dust,

and Dave, the first of all my friends
to challenge God's existence in the ring
or anywhere – God could pick the time and place
and Dave would knock Him senseless,
send Him on a stretcher back to Neverland,
the sleepy little hollow in our soul
as Dave defined the tired search for Heaven
that should have been called off for pity's sake
the day the first child died, and no god wept.

Yes, I remember Dave:
the brashest, most articulate train-spotter
ever to cop or stink
as we waited for another fix of steam.
He taught me how the clouds are heaven-less
with lines like this:

There is no God, you stupid wanker, none.

Those words stay with me more than Nietzsche now.
A simple truth that children come to know:
God is not in Heaven

and Earth is all there is
and Hell can only be if we create it.

How Dave could be so fat and pull the girls
remains a mystery I never solved,
especially since he wore his shirts so tight
and his belly sagged on faded, beltless jeans
and when he felt the urge to fart, he farted
yet some girls he went with were cool blondes
and all I had to show for my politeness
was the bitter burden of virginity.

Dave, in short, was a rebel in reverse
who did not seem to care about the law
that no guy with a girlfriend goes trainspotting.
He had in every sense the best of both:
while I went home to dream of the day's trains
he went out to drink and have it off.

We shall not see his like again.
I heard he died last Christmas
still fat and still denying God
and loving women, and women loving him.

He summed my love life up quite masterfully:
You ain't never done it, not even close!
Sneering, blunt, but not compassionless
while my first love, a Winnie Niner, passed;
I took her number, and looked her up
in my neat and tidy record book.
I thought she was a cop, but found she stank.
We'd seen her here before on May 1st –
less and less is new as you grow old.

Cop? asked Dave, with immaculate indifference.
Stink, I wearily replied.
Just like your fucking sex life, then.
He laughed, and took a swig of beer,
and my sad hand sank in a clump of moss
dampened by the dawn, and not yet dry
but I renounced the macho urge to lie,
admitted to the crime of purity
and humbly asked if Dave could help me up
the impure path to full hormonal joy —
with girls, I mean.

You're too fucking nice,
was his impure advice.
Did no one tell you, Gatsby?
Nice guys don't get laid.

True enough,
but the time would come
after trains,
even for me,
a year from then
in a sort of Eden
behind the church
where I, too, came
because I told my love I'd be a priest.

I stumbled on a primrose path to sex:
once you say you choose to be a virgin
and give yourself to God instead of them
certain women take that as an insult
to their beauty and deific charm.
Virginity is neither here nor there

but celibacy chosen represents
a challenge thrown down by some haughty male
who must be put in his place, and in hers.

So, once I chose to be a lifelong virgin
and most of terraced Latchford knew my choice,
my fate was sealed:
the more I said I wasn't into sex
the louder sex came knocking at my door,
until I had to open.

Qualis pontifex pereo, I groaned
inwardly that Christmas night.
Te rappelles-tu, Barbara?
But, let's get back to trains.

The Arches were a wonder of my world.
That breathless sense of power, speed and grace
gave me my teenage high
when other highs were more in vogue:
I saw the blue Mallard flash by,
the Flying Scot, the Robin Hood,
the Master Cutler, the Pines Express,
the Golden Arrow, the Waverley,
the Lakes Express, the Talisman,
the Palatine, and, slowest of them all,
the William Shakespeare.

And then a man called Beeching
who saw no point in beauty
came like a leech into my life
and silenced steam forever.

The giants were high maintenance, no doubt,
impossible to justify to bankers
but, for those of us who had a soul
to see a steam train was to love mankind
and gasp in wonder at what we could create
when art and science blend in such perfection.

There's one more thing to say, and then I'm done.

As I put away my Ian Allan
and Dave swigged a final can of beer
before we got to Chester Road
beside the Mersey was a football pitch
planned by the Council with their normal care;
real goal posts, but no net,
the right touchline marked neatly out in white,
the left touchline the Mersey.
No booking was required,
people played there day and night.
The railway towered overhead.
The mystic Arches gave the pitch, to me,
Gladiatorial status.

Dave and I joined in the match
on our way home, with silent male acceptance:
Nod, shrug, point, point, whatever,
and so the metaphor continued.
Dave belly-bullied wingers into touch
while I stood self-protectively in goal,
ducking if the shot was struck too hard,
watching steam trains from a new perspective,
catching an occasional back pass;
though my main job, which gave me group acceptance,

was to pluck the bobbing ball
from the green, infested slime
of the never-bobbing Mersey
and cloy the clay away somehow
before I bowled it back and gave it life.

Those, I suppose, were the days,
and this poem is a line under my life
whose circle is now closed.
The cursor blinks impatiently
but I'm at peace for now, with words.
As I approach old age
(a senseless phrase)
Christ is gone, with all of his disciples
but the Twelve Arches remain
ennobling, as they span the listless Mersey
and when I stand beneath them even now
echoes of time return
with the thunder of a steam train
and the loud philosophy of my dead friend
assaulting my unformed ears, to free my mind,

and on the football field where my past is
the roar of victory is heard again.
It doesn't last, but it was there:
a moment is a moment, for all that.
A goal is scored, and I, too old to even stand in goal,
look up, then down, and at the field below
where the game goes on.

The Arches are a living church.
The burden that they bear is purposeful
as it was when I was young

and they contain my past.
I stand there now, and feel such joy,
a wide-eyed, godless Altar Boy,
as a steam train passes overhead
to wake and resurrect the dead
and cover me with dislodged dust
that acts like incense on my soul –
and, as I breathe the ash of what I was
I feel, but do not fear, mortality.

Circle Nine: Fox Covert

Fox Covert's where my mother sleeps.
The sleep we do not wake from.
The panoramic view, unmatched.
The cost of graves not bad at all,
since it's a seller's market.

I never thought that Warrington
could look so lovely and alive,
cradled in a prehistoric valley.
I never saw till now the context of my birth.
It took a death to show me.

All I need to do is lift my eyes;
instead of dying towns and rusted steel
I see the sculpted land that they are part of
and understand the power of Ascension.

Nothing is ugly when seen from on high.
There's beauty in pollution from afar:
the Fiddler's Ferry chimney stacks
my father helped to build
smoke serenely out of time
in Widnes, where Paul Simon wept.

That Protestant monstrosity
Liverpool Cathedral
is, thankfully, a little dot:
Fox Covert shrinks to nothingness
its all-too-solid arches.

How dull the Church of England is,
how sad its attempt to glorify God
there, where the Mersey dies.

At the other end of Hope Street, though,
that tribute to Man's madness
the Catholic Wedding Cake
becomes the dot's twin sister,
the carnival of glass I love,
no match for this short distance.
Fox Covert is in Stockton Heath
where those who've 'made it' live,
not far from Warrington itself
to show they remain
northern in name
though southern in prosperity and ego.

The house my mum was paid to clean
lies just five minutes from her grave.
I think she walked to Stockton Heath from Latchford;
there and back, there and back.
I wonder what she thought on that strange journey
and why her thoughts became my memories.

But, here's the thing I really want to say:

on the day my mum was buried
my dad looked manfully into the grave,
praised its depth and sureness of construction,
and told me there was room for me
when New Jersey wears me out
and, indeed, I've no desire
to spend eternity in the Garden State
as far from Eden as I am from home.

Vectus, Vectus, Vectus, Vectus.

Wait, ein augenblick!
Does any of this matter?
What is family? What is place?
What is distance? What is time?
Here are my dark thoughts:

you're never lonely in a grave
while bankers own the land,
though it takes a hundred years
they'll finally turf you out.

I prophesise
in a century or so
when land is being fought for
and graves are status symbols,
assuming no-one's visited for years,
my family grave will be foreclosed
and auctioned off,
our bones and dust disposed of
to make way for the rich
and the New Dead who'll replace us.

All of this will come to pass.
All of this is just the circle closing:
my paternal and maternal stumps,
the Farquhars and Kilgannons,
were both thrown off the land
and never kicked against the pricks
who dispossessed them.
So, what could be more natural for us
than to be dispossessed again in death?

None of this matters, and yet it does.
I, who believe in little now,
still feel affronted
by the future treatment of my bones.
Though it dissolves into the air
life should have some importance.

I had a dream
(*have* has long been taken)
and here it is, though now I am awake:

the family grave was open,
my coffin on the top
(in life, in death,
last in first out)
and skeleton exposed.

I saw a tall man dressed in white,
a publisher, perhaps,
or undertaker – who can tell? –
pick up the skull that made this poem
and bowl it down Fox Covert.

So, off I set on my last journey
through the thickets,
bouncing over hedges,
swerving through the High Street,
running every red I could
past puzzled cars that stopped themselves;
and on I flew, across the Ship Canal,
back to where I came from.

I left a fragment of my skull
in a pothole on the Causeway
where I watched the Wire lose,
frozen by the rain and time
at the Railway End.

Keep right on to the end of the road,
I heard my mother sing
and passed another awful church:
St. James's, to the right,

and now, I had to climb a hill
up the steep Bridge Foot incline
and roll towards the river which impelled me,
driven by momentum from the grave,

I wobbled through the Bridge Foot traffic,
rolled across the parapet
and, seeing Cromwell's pock-marked face,
fell into the Mersey with a *plop,*
landing softly in the silt,
and waited, as I waited when alive.

Nothing happened for a while.
The river's so much older than I am
and I, polite and shy in death,
waited for her to speak first.

What took you so long?
she finally said.
Diffidence,
I replied.

What do you want from me?
she went on.
Answers,
I suggested.

She closed her mouth, and spoke:

When I was a girl, she said,
the Romans worshipped me.
Now that I've grown old
if people even notice me
they see me as a sewer;
but I remember you,
you used to stand up there
and look at me with love.

Pity, I replied.

I'm so weary of the Irish Sea,
she said,
and salt.
I've seen too much and grown too old.
I think the river-time is over.
The time is ripe for both of us
to rest and die together here –
but let's refuse to move towards our death
the journey to the sea is so clichéd.

Taking my silence for consent, she invoked the Earth:

I, the Mersey, being of sound mind,
though my body's shape-shocked,

renounce herein the salt of Liverpool
in favour of this unsung town
and this poet who was born here
who still has no idea
how out of time and place he's always been.

I, the Mersey, being of sound mind,
and weary of the circles I've created,
per omnia saecla saeclorum,
as they used to say
hereby choose to die in Warrington;
inland, and so forgo a bitter ending.

I, the Mersey, being of sound mind,
announce the end of water, and the world.
May every other river of calm course
soon follow me.
Our time is finished here.

She gathered all her strength for the finale
and I sank down and entered her at last:

To hell with Liverpool, the Mersey said,
I'm staying here in Warrington with you.
I'll die with you, so you don't feel alone.
You'll be a boy again, and I your source.
We'll trace the final circle for old time's sake.
Be there. Da sein.
Willst du mit,
mein kleines kind?
Wie wünschenswert ist ein liebestod.

Being just a skull, I simply nodded
and the Mersey, motionless and dead
watched with me, and waited

and, when the vision – the augenblick – advanced
as it always does, and always will
I heard a voice I knew could not be God
whisper with a mother's tender warmth
to the sleeping child we all become:

Rest, now, little poet.
Soon we'll both be dust.